John Bell

WILD MUSHROOM FIELD GUIDE AND COOKBOOK

A COMPLETE GUIDE TO FORAGING WILD MUSHROOMS AND PREPARE EASY AND DELICIOUS RECIPES.

Table of Content

Introduction

Wondering what all of those strange-looking mushrooms are and how to tell the good ones from the bad? You've come to the right place! This field guide covers common varieties like morels, chanterelle, and mushrooms. It also shows you how to identify edible mushrooms that can be found in your backyard—and tells you how to cook them up with some tasty recipes.

Most people don't know what wild mushrooms are or when they should be eaten. Many have been so misinformed that they think that anything from the forest ground is edible. This, of course, is not true, and it's actually pretty dangerous.

Mushrooms are delicious and nutritious food that can be found pretty much anywhere. There are, however, some mushrooms that can be deadly if eaten raw or contaminated with toxins. Eating the wrong kind of mushroom could make you sick or worse - it's important to know what kind of mushroom you're picking!

Mushrooms are a diverse group of organisms that only began to be recognized as a separate kingdom during the 1800s. They all belong to the Fungi, which is a large group of organisms that can be difficult to define with any one characteristic. They are probably best known for the properties that distinguish them from other plants, but they also have some specialized characteristics. Because they reproduce through spores, they lack stems and leaves and instead rely entirely on the structure of their fruit body(s) for their support and nutrition.

Modern mushrooms grow in close association with their environment. They are typically found growing on dead trees or rotting logs and can be very difficult to tell apart from other fungus-like organisms. The most common mushroom species found in the wild are members of the genus Agaricus, though there are many others. Although most of these mushrooms have been identified by their gills, as they mature, they develop various colored spines that make it much easier to identify them.

Mushrooms grow in association with a wide variety of other life forms, which helps to keep them hidden from us. They tend to grow on decaying or dead wood, so like many fungi,, they have a very close symbiotic relationship with other organisms. The wood that mushrooms consume is often decayed wood from trees that have died but have not yet been completely broken down by the action of fungi. In exchange, mushrooms provide the fungi with the food they need to undergo the process of decomposition and break down the dead timber.

Understanding how mushrooms grow and interact with their environment can help you identify them more easily when you find them in nature. Mushrooms are very widespread, so it is possible to track them down pretty much anywhere.

The main parts of the mushroom that you need to identify are its cap, the stem, and the gills. Each of these parts is used to identify a particular kind of mushroom. You can look for several things when identifying mushrooms, and their different size, coloration, and texture can all help you tell them apart from one another. You should also try to see what kind of fruit body they have - some have spherical ones or flat ones with gills on one side. This will also help distinguish them from other forms of fungus that have features similar to mushrooms.

The mushroom cap is the most obvious part and will be the easiest to identify. The cap can be different colors depending on how much light it has been exposed to, but it is typically either white, brown or reddish. Cap coloration is often used to distinguish different mushrooms from one another. Different mushrooms have caps that can range in size and shape too. The stem of a mushroom also plays an important role in helping you identify it by its odor, texture, or appearance when broken or picked up.

The first thing you need to know is that, in most cases, if a wild mushroom is completely white, it's not safe to eat. This is probably one of the most important things to keep in mind because many different mushrooms are completely white and almost all toxic. This is why when we were kids, our parents told us not to eat any mushrooms that were brightly colored or had any color at all. The reason for this warning was that some of the most toxic mushrooms known, like the death cap, share the same characteristics as non-toxic mushrooms like the popular button mushroom.

The second thing you need to know is that the shape of a mushroom can be very important in determining whether or not it's safe to eat. There are countless mushrooms out there, and all of them can be found in different shapes and sizes, so this is definitely one of the most important factors for picking off safe ones. Also, keep in mind that a mushroom can change color, texture, and size depending on when and where it's cultivated. So by knowing what type of forest environment the mushrooms were raised in will also help you determine how much risk you should take when eating them.There are many wild mushrooms out there, yet only a few are truly toxic. The other ones are safe to eat and make for great additions to your favorite dishes. The most common way of preparing wild mushrooms is simply boiling them with some butter. This is especially true for the button and cremini mushrooms you can find at the grocery store.

Sometimes, though, you might want a more exotic dish. And we all know that the way you choose a dish depends on what's in season. However, what about when there are certain mushrooms in the season that you want to try that are not found anywhere else? And how can you identify whether or not these species are safe for consumption?

Mushroom Foraging

When some folks go hiking and spot a mushroom in the forest, they simply go in the other direction. People who hate seeing mushrooms spot one growing on their lawn, kick it, or chemically terminate it.

The dislike these people have for mushrooms is understandable as many mushrooms are poisonous, and only a few are edible. However, if you can learn how to identify edible mushrooms, you can begin to enjoy the benefits that mushrooms provide.

How to Identify Mushrooms

Some mushrooms are lovely to eat, many others are toxic, causing severe or temporary discomfort, and most mushrooms are unpalatable or tasteless. The challenge is how to identify the few edible mushrooms.

There are thousands of mushroom species worldwide, with some having strange shapes, while some don't look like mushrooms. As you venture further into the mushroom kingdom, you begin to see how the world of mushrooms is complex and intricate.

However, identifying edible mushrooms is not an impossible task. There are processes to follow, as discussed below.

The Correct Process of Mushroom Identification

The mushroom identification process starts with knowing the characteristics of various mushrooms. This stage can come easily if your focus is to identify a few mushrooms.

However, if you want to expand into identifying a wide variety of mushrooms, you will need a mushroom identification book.

There are several mushrooms in the wild that area lookalike like some edible mushrooms, and you can easily mistake them for what they are not. The mushroom identification book serves as your guide to differentiate between the lookalike and the edible mushrooms.

Aside from that, these are four stages to identifying any mushroom;

- **Observation**

Any mushroom will willingly give its identity away if you know what to look for. What then should you look for in a mushroom?

Begin by looking at its cap. Take note of its length, width, color, and shape.

Also, check under the cap. Note its distinctive features such as color, spacing, strip attachment, etc.

The next thing is to check the stem. Check for striations, stripes, rings, and other identifying features.

Its substrate is also an important thing to check. Where and what is the mushroom growing on?

And lastly, confirm the season of growth. Mushrooms grow at different times in the year. Check to see if it's growing at the right time. If not, it is most likely a lookalike.

- **Examination**

When examining mushrooms, what you do is smell them, feel them, and taste them.

Edible mushrooms have nice smells that can help you identify them. If it doesn't smell great, then it's most likely not an edible mushroom.

It's also important to note how the mushroom feels when you touch it. Edible mushrooms usually feel smooth, fuzzy, slimy, and pleasant to touch.

Lastly, go ahead to taste the mushroom. Cut a portion of it and place it on your tongue then, spit it out. If it tastes bitter, it's an indication to stay away from it. And, don't worry, it won't harm you if you spit it out.

- **Use Key**

At this point, you bring out the mushroom identification book to check the characteristics as described in the book. If it's not what you think it is, it might just be another edible mushroom.

- **Check and Confirm Answers**

Finally, if you have observed, examined, and cross-checked, it is time to decide based on the characteristics you have found. Note that if it is not 100 percent in agreement with what the features say, stay away from such mushrooms.

Tips to Identify Poisonous Mushrooms

There is no single rule that guides the identification of poisonous mushrooms. But, when you come across a mushroom, a few defining characteristics could help you determine if it's toxic or not.

Take note of the following tips to avoid picking mushrooms that may be poisonous by mistake;

- Don't pick mushrooms with white gills
- Avoid mushrooms with a skirt or ring on the stalk
- Avoid mushrooms that have red caps or stalks

These are not definitive as some edible mushrooms can also exhibit some of these characteristics. However, when you notice them, it's a good indication that you need to stay away from such mushrooms.

You may miss out on a tasty mushroom, but you are at least sure that you won't get sick from the consumption of a poisonous mushroom. Note that, for safety reasons, you shouldn't eat any mushroom, if you are not 100 percent sure about its edibility.

Mushroom Cultivation

You love hiking and walking in the woods. But, you don't want to go through the stress of foraging for edible mushrooms every time you want to spice your meal with them. Mushroom cultivation is the answer you seek.

Mushroom cultivation is one sure way to get the type of mushrooms you need either on a small scale or commercial scale. Mushroom foraging is a gamble, especially if you are new to the game. Even experts sometimes make mistakes.

But, when you grow your mushrooms, you can't get it wrong.

Also, those who love a particular type of mushroom may find it difficult to find it in the grocery store. In such a case, growing your mushroom colony is the best solution to the quick access you desire.

With a few tools and the proper growing system, you can have more than enough mushrooms anytime you need them.

Essentials of Mushroom Cultivation

Cultivated mushrooms are edible mushrooms that you grow on decaying organic substances.

You should know the classification of the different mushroom species based on how they tap nutrients to understand the essentials needed for mushroom cultivation. The classifications are;

- **Saprobic**

A saprobic plant grows on dead organic substances. Saprobic edibles are valued for their food and medicine.

They require a constant supply of organic matters suitable to sustain their production in their cultivated form. Otherwise, it can be a limiting factor in production.

- **Symbiotic**

A symbiotic mushroom grows in association with other organisms. They are mostly found in the wild on trees.

The relationship works in that the mushroom helps the tree gather extensive water catchments and help deliver nutrients from the soil that the tree cannot access.

- **Parasitic or Pathogenic**

Most pathogenic fungi cause diseases to plants. Only a small number of such fungi are edible.

These are the three major classifications of the thousands of mushroom species.

Therefore, mushrooms species are primarily cultivated in two ways:

1. *Composted Substrate*

Composted substrates are organic matters from substances like rice and wheat straw, hay, corn curb, composted manure, water hyacinth, and several other agricultural by-products, including banana leaves and coffee husks.

2. Woody Substrate

This method majorly involves substances such as sawdust, wood logs, or any by-products of wood.

Six Critical Steps in Mushroom Cultivation

The basic concept in mushroom production or cultivation begins with some mushroom spores. These spores grow into mycelium, expanding into massive stored up energy and sufficient mass to support the final phase in the mushroom reproduction cycle.

The formation of mushroom or fruiting bodies is the last phase of the mushroom reproduction cycle. From start to finish, a complete cycle usually takes between two to three months, depending on the mushroom species.

The vital generic steps in the production process are;

1. Identify and Clean Cultivation Space

You'll need to decide on the room or building to use for cultivation and cleaning the room. Ensure that you choose a place to control the moisture, temperature, and sanitary condition. Those are the conditions that determine the growth of the spores.

2. Growing Medium

There are two primary growing mediums for mushroom cultivation, as stated above. Choose the growing medium you find convenient to work with or suit the growing environment you have chosen. Then, store the raw ingredients clean and protect them from rain.

3. Pasteurize Medium

You'll need to pasteurize or sterilize the medium and table or bags the mushrooms will grow. This sterilization ensures you exclude other fungi from growing on the same platform, thereby competing for nutrients. When the mushroom begins to grow, it colonizes the substance and fights off all competitions.

4. Seeding

The next step is to seed the bed with spawn when you've done all that.

5. Coordinated Growing Environment

This stage is the most challenging because it is at this point that most of the work is done. You need to maintain optimal moisture, temperature, hygiene, and other conditions that make for the proper growth of mycelium and fruiting. You'll also need to regularly add water to the substrate to raise the moisture content.

6. Harvesting and Recycle

Harvesting is the last stage of the mushroom reproduction process. You process your mushrooms for eating or package for selling at this point. After this, you clean the room and start over again.

Species Selection

Most mushroom species only bear fruits in an environment of about 20 degrees Celsius. Therefore, you will hardly find one growing in a temperate climate. You should stimulate the growing environment temperature to cultivate mushrooms.

Aside from that, the other factors to consider in choosing species to grow to include:

1. Availability of Waste materials for Growing

Not all mushrooms fruit, in the same substrate. You should determine the type of substrate you have available before choosing the mushroom species.

2. Condition of the Environment

Different species have environmental conditions in which they thrive. As explained earlier, most mushroom species have difficulty growing in temperate regions. If you reside in a tropical zone, you can only grow varieties that survive in such areas.

3. The Expertise You Have

Some species don't grow easily because of the expertise needed to produce them. If you do not know how to grow such species and don't have an expert that you can consult, it's best to start with simpler species like oysters. Shiitake and maitake mushrooms are also viable options.

4. The Resources You Have

Aside from having enough waste materials needed to support the species you choose, you also need to consider the availability of the resources required to grow such species.

If you'll need to coordinate the environmental temperature for the species to survive, do you have what it takes to achieve that? Also, consider other required resources and judge if you dare to grow such species.

5. Demand in the Market

You might not worry about market demand if you only grow for personal consumption. On the other hand, if you're growing for commercial use, you must consider the market demand for such species.

Some people prefer some particular species with an unrepentant bias to some other species. You might need to do a market survey to determine the best mushroom species to grow within your catchment area.

Key Species and the Cultivation Methods

Here are some of the commonly cultivated edible mushroom species accepted globally.

White Button Mushroom (Agaricus Bisporus)

The white button is top on the list of cultivated edible mushrooms by farmers worldwide, most grown in temperate regions. You can grow the mushroom in a composted substrate.

You will need higher technology systems because a consistent temperature of 14 to 18 degrees Celsius is required when growing the Agaricus Bisporus. Though it can grow at a higher temperature, it needs to grow in an environment within that temperature to get the best of its fruiting process.

Oyster Mushroom (Pleurotus ostreatus)

Oyster mushrooms are easier to cultivate compared to other mushroom species. Therefore, they are the best choice for inexperienced mushroom farmers. Besides, their farming process helps utilize farm waste, consequently becoming an integral part of a sustainable agricultural system.

Cultivators normally grow Oysters on tree logs. People started growing them on sawdust, rice, or wheat straw, and other variety of waste materials having high-cellulose recently. Growing oysters on high-cellulose waste materials reduce its fruiting period to about two months.

The cultivation process involves placing the substrate in a plastic bag and keeping it cool and dark. As the mycelium grows on the substrate, you should cut an opening in the bag, allowing the fruiting bodies to develop.

Shiitake Mushrooms (Lentinus edodes)

Shiitake mushrooms grow easily and require few resources. You can grow shiitakes, both outdoors and indoors. You can cultivate it on a log when outdoors, and when indoors, you grow it on sawdust or in bags.

The cultivation system that involves sawdust speeds up the fruiting cycle and increases the returns you get. However, it needs more skillful management than when logs are used.

When you cultivate your mushrooms using logs, the fruiting bodies appear faster based on the diameter of the substrate logs. How long the product will last depends on how dense the wood is.

Paddy Straw Mushrooms (Volvariella volvacea)

Paddy Straw Mushrooms are cultivated along with rice production. However, you can also grow it on substrates in addition to paddy straw, cotton waste, rice straw, oil palm bunch waste, and dried banana leaves. However, this method yields fewer returns.

In many rural areas, mushroom cultivators just leave thoroughly moistened paddy straw under trees and wait for the mushrooms to grow.

Assets Required for Mushroom Cultivation

Mushroom cultivation demands activities that people with diverse interests, various needs, and specific capabilities can do. Find the crucial assets you need to cultivate mushrooms below.

1. Natural Assets

Land and climatic conditions play a small role in mushroom cultivation, which makes it possible for farmers with limited areas to join in the enterprise. Also, the unpredictable production that plagues the typical farming system does not apply to mushroom cultivation.

Access to sufficient and locally-sourced spore substrate is an essential determinant for the success of mushroom cultivation. How easy is it to get agricultural by-products, logs, or sawdust as the mushroom species requires, and how cheap is it? You can also get spores from mature fruiting bodies or buy them from local facilities.

2. Human Assets

Human assets mean the skills, knowledge, and ability to work needed to do a line of work. Mushroom cultivation requires little human effort, and you can operate them as an addition to other tasks.

Because it isn't labor-intensive, people with disabilities can also do mushroom farming and carry out the required tasks. People with mental disabilities can also grow mushrooms because a majority of the tasks involved are repetitive.

3. Physical Assets

The physical equipment needed to grow mushrooms depend on how large the production is. However, many of the physical assets for growing mushrooms are inclusive tools. These items are typical needs such as water, transportation, source of energy, and buildings.

Mushrooms grow best in a cool, enclosed building. You can easily maintain environmental elements such as temperature, humidity, moisture level, and proper ventilation in this structure. These conditions allow for proper growth.

4. Financial Assets

The product's sale determines the financial capacity you need for mushroom cultivation. Since you can grow mushrooms on any scale, the financial commitment to begin a mushroom cultivation system need not be huge. Besides, substrates in agricultural by-products or logs are often gotten for free.

Compared to other agricultural and horticultural crops, mushroom cultivation systems allow for harvesting after a short time. You can grow mushrooms and harvest them within two to four months. Small-scale producers find this an advantage.

Nutritional Values of Mushrooms

Though some mushrooms can be poisonous, we cannot discard the fact that they have nutritional and medicinal values. While the nutritional and medicinal values present in mushrooms are different according to the species, see some of the general benefits below.

1. Nutritional Value

Mushrooms add flavor to food, enhancing the taste of bland foods. They are also a valuable source of food in their own right. Fleshy mushrooms can replace meat and have enough nutrients to compete with several vegetables.

Mushrooms can be added to a meal for a balanced diet, which is of great value, especially to people in developing countries. They are a good source of vitamin B, C, D and several other minerals like copper, phosphorus, potassium, and iron.

They also provide carbohydrates and are low in cholesterol, fiber, and starch. Furthermore, they are a good source of protein. Mushrooms reportedly contain between 19 to 35 percent of protein, higher than kidney beans.

2. Medicinal Value

In addition to the nutritional values, mushrooms have medicinal benefits of polysaccharides, which are good for boosting your immune system. Now that there's recent promotion of functional foods and focus on other products "that is more than food," mushrooms are a perfect fit into that category.

Mushrooms have routinely been added to Chinese traditional medicines in history. Now, more than six percent of edible mushrooms play a part in many of today's health tonics and herbal formulas.

Cleaning and PreservationTechnique

There is little doubt that foraging is one of the most fun and magical hobbies to follow. It's fun to think of exploring unknown territories, discovering exotic mushrooms, having your wicker basket overflowing with mushrooms, returning home to look at your collection with awe and happiness. It's exciting cooking and eating the delicious dishes, sharing them with your friends and family, and everything related to mushroom foraging.

After you finish everything listed above, you look at your basket and realize you still have so many mushrooms left, and now you are stumped. What to do with such a big collection? Wasting them is not an option because it is not the behavior of an ethical mushroom forager.

Well, preserving is a great option because you can keep your collected mushrooms for a longer time and use them as additions to multiple dishes. In fact, preserving foraged mushrooms is a bounteous thing to do for all mushroom foragers. The process of preserving mushrooms starts with cleaning them.

How to Clean Mushrooms

Cleaning mushrooms can be quite a chore considering that many varieties, especially the popular ones like chanterelles, carry a lot of litter from the forest floor. Here are some tips on cleaning mushrooms with water:

Put a few of them (do them in small batches) into a colander with small perforations. Run them under tap water directly from the faucet. Use a small brush to remove the dirt from the mushrooms even as they are being washed with running water. Once your mushrooms are cleaned thoroughly, please put them in a bigger colander with larger perforations for draining.

Once the mushrooms are completely drained of water, spread them on a single towel and leave them overnight to ensure all the moisture is removed and they are dried. Use the following tips to clean mushrooms before cooking them:

1. Before you rinse your mushroom, slice them to your desired size. Halve, quarter, or slice your mushrooms before you clean them in water so that you get more

surface area resulting in cleaner mushrooms than if you tried to rinse them wholly without cutting.

2. Place the mushrooms inside a colander and space them out so that each piece gets ample exposure to water for rinsing.

3. Small varieties like the button mushrooms just need a quick rinse to remove all dirt.

4. Ensure the faucet runs at medium pressure and the water is at room temperature.

5. Then, dry off the rinsed mushrooms, examine each piece thoroughly, and cut off those parts where dirt or mold could not be removed by rinsing.

6. For mushrooms that should not be water-rinsed, you can use a damp paper towel to rub off any caked-on sediments. Alternatively, you can use a fresh toothbrush dipped in a bit of water to do so.

Different Methods of Preserving Mushrooms

Some of the common ways of preserving mushrooms include:

- Drying
- Freezing
- Powdering
- Tincturing
- Pickling
- Making mushroom ketchup

Let us look at each of them in a bit of detail:

Drying Mushrooms

When you thoroughly dry mushrooms, you can keep them longer than fresh ones. For example, if you end up with a lot of mushrooms when you go foraging during fall, then you can simply dry them up. In the dried state, you can use them right through the winter months as well.

There are various methods of drying mushrooms:

- Lay them out in the sun after cleaning them thoroughly.

- Place them in a dehydrator overnight at a temperature of around 115 to 120 degrees F. By morning; the mushrooms will become a little crispy like fries.

Use these tips for drying your mushrooms (typically, you will get 1.5 ounces of dried mushrooms from one pound of fresh ones):

- Slice the mushrooms thinly. The slices should not be more than ½-inch in thickness. The thumb rule is this. The thicker the flesh, the thinner your slice should be. Then, you can dry them out in the sun using any of these methods:
- String the sliced mushrooms and hang them to dry in an airy room, which gets a lot of sunlight. Alternately, you can put them out into direct sunlight, especially when the weather is warm.
- You can spread out the slices on a wire screen and place the mushrooms on a heat register to dry slowly.
- The trick is to dry mushrooms until they break like a cracker. If the mushroom only bends or still seems moist, then you must continue the drying process until it becomes 'cracker dry.'

- Simply lay them in a single layer on a sheet of newspaper and put them out to dry. You would need to repeat this process every day, occasionally turning the sliced mushrooms over until they are completely dry. It is important not to crowd the mushrooms.

It is better not to dry mushrooms in an oven because it requires a lot of continuous monitoring. If you let them dry in an oven unchecked for very long, then your mushrooms can become extremely hard and inedible as it gets challenging to rehydrate them. You can store the completely dried mushrooms in an airtight container with a small packet of desiccant to prevent moisture absorption in the future as well.

Attach a label on the container with the following details:

- Type of mushroom
- Date collected
- Place collected
- Date preserved
- Any other important information

Next, freeze them airtight container for a week to ensure any microbes that might have made their way into the mushrooms during the dehydration process. After a week of freezing it, remove the container and store it in a dry place.

You can also use a food hydrator to dry and preserve mushrooms. Arrange the sliced mushrooms on the racks of the food hydrator, ensuring they are not overcrowded. Slow drying at a lower temperature (about 150 degrees C) over a longer period is better than quickly drying at high temperatures. Higher temperatures tend to damage mushrooms and their nutrients.

The process for rehydrating these dried mushrooms is very simple. Soak them in warm water for about 15-20 minutes, and your mushrooms are ready for use. Also, don't discard the water in which the mushrooms were soaked because it will absorb the flavors of the dried mushrooms. Therefore, you can use it in cooking your dishes. It would be like a mushroom stock.

You can use the drying method for morels, Shiitake, etc. Black trumpet mushrooms (found abundantly in the northeastern parts of North America) are among the best mushrooms to be used in the dried form. They get a smoky, aromatic, and pleasantly fruity flavor when dry. They can be harvested during summer and used in the dry form right through winter.

The advantage of drying mushrooms include:

- Drying is the best method to preserve the flavor for a long time. In fact, drying intensifies the flavor of many mushroom species.
- It is very easy and convenient to store dried mushrooms. There is no need for any special equipment.
- The disadvantages of drying mushrooms are:
- Drying is likely to change the texture of mushrooms, making them quite tough.
- Aromas are often lost in the drying process.
- Rehydration does not restore the texture of mushrooms to earlier levels.
- Using dehydrating machines can be expensive and elaborate.

Freezing Mushrooms

Button mushrooms are great to preserve through freezing methods. You can leave the small-sized button mushrooms as they are and slice the larger ones. The mushrooms for freezing must not be longer than about 1 inch. You can use any one of the following methods to freeze mushrooms:

- Sauté them in a little bit of butter or olive oil. Then cool them to room temperature and then transfer the mushrooms to plastic containers or freezer bags.

- You can steam the mushrooms over boiling water or a steaming pot. After about 10 minutes of steaming, cool your mushrooms, and transfer them to containers or bags.

- You can also blanch the mushrooms before freezing them. Whichever method you use to cook your mushrooms for not more than 10 minutes, you must cool them completely before transferring them to freezer packs or plastic containers.

The container's label must have more detail than just that it's dried mushrooms. That information details whether the mushrooms were sautéed, blanched, or steamed and the date of the cooking process. Matsutake, Verpa, morels, pig's ears, and chanterelles are great to preserve by the freezing method.

The advantages of blanching and freezing partially cooked mushrooms as a preserving method are:

- Blanching is a great way to clean the mushrooms as well as prevent them from becoming mushy.
- Dirt and sand are all removed through blanching without affecting the flavors of the frozen end product.
- This preservation process is convenient for large quantities in a short period.
- You can just put frozen mushrooms into your soups as pre-thawing is not necessary.

One of the biggest disadvantages of blanching and freezing is that the frozen mushrooms are not suitable for frying, sautéing, or crisping mushrooms.

The advantages of steaming and freezing mushrooms include:

- Steaming is quite convenient.

- The end frozen product is more versatile than the blanched and frozen end product.
- The texture and flavors are excellently preserved.
- The disadvantages of the steaming and freezing method are:
- Steaming takes more time and effort than the blanching process.
- Dirt and sand are not removed as well as in the blanching process. Therefore, you must select only those thoroughly cleaned mushrooms for this process. You should use other freezing methods for others.
- The advantages of sautéing and freezing method of mushroom preservation are:
- Convenient and easy, the texture and taste of the mushrooms preserved in this way are the best of the three.
- The quality of texture and flavor is not retained for as long as the other two methods.

Pickling Mushrooms

For pickling mushrooms, you will need some extra ingredients. Also, mason jars with bands and lids work best for storing your pickled mushrooms. It is done that you sterilize the jars before storing your pickled mushrooms. Here is a simple method to sterilize mason jars:

- Put the jar in boiling water for about 10 minutes.
- Then, remove the jar from the hot water with a pair of tongs, and place it on a clean towel to dry.

Other ingredients needed for pickling mushrooms are (the given measurements are suitable for six cups of mushrooms):

- o 10 Peppercorns
- o Sprigs of thyme
- o Dried hot chili
- o Garlic cloves
- o Kosher salt
- o White vinegar
- o Olive oil

- Granulated sugar

Clean the mushrooms well. Using a variety of mushrooms is a great way to make the pickle highly flavorful. Boil the mushrooms for a little more time than you would in drying or freezing the mushrooms. About 15 minutes would do.

Bring to boil all the other ingredients mentioned above in water so that you can get a nicely-spiced sauce. When this sauce is nicely boiled, pour it over the cooked mushrooms. Fill the sterilized jars with the pickled mushrooms and pour some more sauce until the mushrooms are fully covered.

Seal the lid on the filled mason jar and allow it to cool to room temperature, after which you must refrigerate the pickled mushrooms. You can use a variety of spices and herbs to pickle your mushrooms depending on your likes/dislikes and how each spice marries with each mushroom.

The advantages of pickling mushrooms are:

- Pickle broths used to marinate mushrooms intensify the flavors. Therefore, pickling is excellent to preserve bland varieties.

- It is relatively easy to pickle mushrooms at home.

- The disadvantages of the pickling method are:

- You require proven recipes, and it is imperative that you strictly adhere to the recipes.

- It is not a great method to experiment with because wrong pickling can result in food poisoning.

Preserving the extra harvested mushrooms is good for you and a reflection of your respect for the fruits of nature. By preserving picked mushrooms, you are essentially telling Mother Nature that you value every little thing she gives you. Therefore, make sure you don't pick more than you need, and if you do, for some reason, ensure nothing is wasted.

Cooking Technique

Mushrooms are a popular ingredient in culinary traditions across the globe, so if you love home cooking, you may be excited about preparing tried-and-tested recipes with the species you find. One thing you may not have imagined is having more mushrooms on your hands than you can immediately use. Read on to discover why mushrooms should be cooked and learn a few useful tips for preserving excess mushrooms.

Why Is It Important to Cook Mushrooms?

Fresh mushrooms can be used in various dishes ranging from pasta right through to soups and stews. Many are also delicious grilled or fried, and almost all taste amazing sautéed with butter and either garlic or shallots. Although experimenting with different recipes is fine, bear in mind that mushrooms should be cooked thoroughly before eating—they should never be consumed raw. One reason is that mushrooms have tough cell walls and can be indigestible if they are not cooked.

Heating also allows a mushroom's nutrients to break free, enabling you to access an array of vitamins and minerals. This includes protein, B vitamins, riboflavin (excellent for red blood cells), niacin (which can promote digestive health), and pantothenic acid (which can help your skin look younger). Cooking mushrooms can also make irritants, allergens, natural toxins, and even bugs in raw edible mushrooms harmless to human health.

Avoid Alcohol When Trying Mushrooms for the First Time

Before you have a glass of wine or any other alcoholic beverage with specific mushroom species, make sure you are not allergic to them. Alcohol can make allergic reactions to mushrooms worse. Furthermore, mushrooms from the genus Coprinus (also known as shaggy mane) might have negative effects when combined with alcohol. If you consume these mushrooms within three days of consuming alcohol, you may get symptoms such as nausea, vomiting, sweating, tingling, palpitations, and diarrhea...

Steaming Mushrooms

To stop mushrooms from becoming darker during the steaming process, soak them first in a little lemon juice or a blend of citric acid and water (use around 15ml per liter), leaving the mushrooms to soak for around five minutes. Then steam according to the times recommended.

- Sliced mushrooms: Three minutes
- Quartered mushrooms: Three and a half minutes
- Button mushrooms: Three and a half minutes
- Whole mushrooms: Five minutes

After steaming the mushrooms, set them aside until they have completely cooled down and flash-freeze them on trays. Once they are completely frozen, remove them gently from the trays and place them in a freezer-proof bag or sealed container, leaving about a centimeter of the bag free and removing as much air as possible before sealing the bag.

To reuse mushrooms once they are frozen, thaw them overnight in the fridge or drop them as-is into your favorite soup or stew.

Sautéing Mushrooms

You can also sauté your mushrooms after slicing them. Heat them up for around five minutes in a pan with butter or your favorite oil. Wait for them to cool down, then flash freeze them and once again, place them in a freezer-safe bag or container as above.

If possible, use a vacuum sealer even if you are opting to freeze mushrooms, as this will help your mushrooms preserve a better texture and avoid freezer burn.

Whipping Up a Delicious Mushroom Dish

Without a doubt, one of the most fulfilling experiences after a day out foraging is preparing a beautiful dish with the goodies you have found. Chefs use mushrooms in an array of healthy, beautifully flavored dishes, ranging from hearty vegan burgers to light-and-airy soufflés. Foragers often say, however, that nothing quite gives mushrooms its rightful place on the table as sautéed mushrooms—which are easy and quick to prepare, yet incredibly tantalizing to the taste buds.

To sauté your mushrooms, ensure they are clean and dry, so they develop a beautiful golden-brown hue in the pan. If you are using sliced or diced mushrooms, ensure that all pieces are more or less the same size to cook equally in the pan. As is the case with high-water vegetables, you need to be wary of overfilling your pan since doing so will cause your product to steam instead of brown.

Heat a cast iron pan slightly and add your chosen oil or butter to start cooking. Add the mushrooms in one layer without stirring them excessively. Flip them over once they have browned until the other side takes on the same appealing hue. Remove the pan from the heat and season your mushrooms with a little salt, additional butter, and lemon zest. Some people also enjoy adding ingredients like white wine, garlic, and thyme once one side is browned. Always add salt after your mushrooms are done since salt pulls out moisture and can cause your mushrooms to steam.

Black Trumpet Mushroom

The scientific name of the black trumpet mushroom is Craterellus Fallax. At first glance, these mushrooms may not look edible, but they have an incredibly delicious flavor that will pleasantly surprise you. These trumpet-shaped black mushrooms are tricky to spot especially given their shape and color. They are shaped like a skyward-facing trumpet and have a deadwood-like appearance. These mushrooms are incredibly scaly on the inside and quite fragile. So, ensure you are extremely careful while handling them. The stalk of these mushrooms is quite thick close to the base, and it doesn't have any gills. They also tend to grow in clusters.

They are commonly found in warmer climates between July and September. Don't forget to check for layers on the forest floor because these mushrooms are usually hidden there. These mushrooms can also be dried and stored. These mushrooms are rich in a variety of vitamins, including Vitamin B12. They are considered to improve heart and skin health, promote weight loss, and reduce cholesterol levels.

Chanterelles Mushroom

With more than 15 different species, Chanterelles are another common variety of wild mushrooms found abundantly across North America. They are also available in plenty in Central America, Africa, and Eurasia. Chanterelles typically grow in coniferous forests. But you can also find them in certain specific species in grasslands and particular locations in mountainous birch and beech forests.

These mushrooms usually grow in clumps among the moss. The harvest season for chanterelles starts from late summer and extends up to December, depending on the location and the species. The distinctive characteristics of chanterelles include:

- Funnel-shaped golden or meaty yellow mushrooms.
- The gill-like ridges under the cap run right along the stem downwards.
- Chanterelles have an earthy, fruity, or woody smell.

Chanterelles have a peppery taste and are quite rich in flavor, turn out excellent dishes that use wines, butter, or cream. Poisonous look-alikes of chanterelles or false chanterelles are darker yellow (almost orange) caps. The caps also have dark centers that fade progressively towards the edges. False chanterelles are rarely fatal. However, they have horrible taste and can also cause stomach problems. Examples of false morels include jack-o-lantern mushrooms.

The ideal weather for the growth of chanterelle mushrooms involves hot and humid days. The days after heavy rains are also very favorable for their growth. Chanterelles take on a reddish-orange color. They are small, but they are not hard to spot due to their bright color. A very wide range of mushroom species can be categorized as chanterelle mushrooms. In the United States, three distinct color groups of chanterelles are very common.

Red chanterelles: these small and thin-fleshed mushrooms sure are a treat for the eyes. They are also called cinnabars. Cinnabars taste like mild notes of apricots mixed with almonds.

Black chanterelles: often referred to as 'black trumpets,' these mushrooms are larger than cinnabars but smaller than orange chanterelles. They, too, are thin-fleshed. Black trumpets are known for their delicious taste. Typically, they are dried, powdered, and cooked in olive oil to create black trumpet oil. This oil is mostly enjoyed with bread.

Orange chanterelles: the orange chanterelles, unlike their name, come in a range of colors, including pink, peach, yellow, and of course, orange. Orange chanterelles have a wide variety of sub-species under them with slightly different shapes, colors, and sizes. In the United States, there are hundreds of closely related yet genetically distinct subspecies of orange chanterelles.

Like black chanterelles, orange chanterelles are also delicious when cooked. They have a subtle taste with hints of apricots and almonds.

Where to find orange chanterelle mushrooms: these mushrooms are found abundantly in the United States. In fact, it is found in all the states except Hawaii as the weather conditions of Hawaii aren't favorable for their growth.

They form a symbiotic relationship with their surrounding trees. This means their host tree feeds them, and they feed their host trees. This is why chanterelles are often found growing in mature and thick forests. They are prominently found around oak, beech, and maple, and sometimes, even evergreen trees.

When chanterelles grow: these mushrooms love hot and humid conditions. Heavy rain will start the growth of chanterelle mushrooms, and within two weeks of rain, you will find prominent growth of chanterelle mushrooms.

What chanterelles look like: the most prominent species of chanterelle mushrooms are the red, black, and orange species. It is very easy to find orange chanterelles because of their abundance and large size. Apart from their colors, almost all chanterelles take on a vase-like shape. The underside of these mushrooms consists of false gills. These false gills fork, unlike true gills that are individual blades. They are found to grow either alone or in small clusters near trees. They give out a very sweet and fruity smell.

It is important to know about their poisonous look-alikes as well. Here are some important look-alikes:

- **Jack-o-lantern mushrooms**: these mushrooms are poisonous. They have a characteristic bright orange color, and their gills have a green glow at night. They grow around dead and decaying trees, mostly found in clusters.

- **False chanterelles**: these mushrooms look very similar to the true chanterelles. It is safe to consume these mushrooms, but some people have reported no side effects despite having consumed these mushrooms, and others have complained of stomach aches and fever. It is best to stay away from these mushrooms. Unlike true chanterelles, these mushrooms have true gills in the underside layer of their cap.

- **Hedgehog mushrooms**: You consume them without any second thoughts if you come across this mushroom. They taste delicious. The catch is that they are much rarer than orange chanterelles. You know you have found hedgehog mushrooms if you see tiny white teeth in the cap's underside. This is where the spores are released.

How to Harvest Chanterelles

Once you have identified chanterelles, it is time to harvest them.

1. Cut the mushrooms at the base of the stem to avoid harming the neighboring clusters and reduce the time you need to clean your mushrooms.
2. Make sure to pick only clean chanterelles and leave behind the ones covered in mud. Plus, the ones you leave behind will give out spores that will grow into fresh chanterelles.
3. It's best to harvest the old and large ones rather than the young and small ones. This ensures that they have produced spores already.

4. Use a filter or a breathable basket while carrying chanterelles to give out spores over the areas they are being carried to. This gives birth to new chanterelle colonies.

5. Do not pluck chanterelles and store them for later use. They will start to go bad within two days. If you keep them refrigerated, they can live up to a week or two.

How to Cook Them

- The first step is to dehydrate them and powder them. Chanterelles are 95% water, which can later be used to add flavor to other dishes.

- Sauté them in butter or oil for twenty minutes. Let them cool and put them in Ziplock bags in the fridge. This method takes up more storage space than dehydrated mushrooms, but the flavor stays in the mushroom for a longer period.

Morels and chanterelles are found abundantly in North America, and even as a novice mushroom forager, you are unlikely to miss them when you are on your hunt.

Chicken of the Wood Mushrooms

Also known as chicken mushrooms, sulfur shelf mushrooms are found growing on adult trees and dead ones, especially on the eastern side of the Rocky Mountains. While the most typical harvest season is summer, they can also be harvested from spring until summer, provided the climate is right for its growth. Identifying characteristics include:

- Sulfur shelf mushrooms do not have gills.
- The upper part of this mushroom is salmon-pink or orange in color, while the lower part is bright yellow.
- They grow in clumps on many trees, but especially on oak trees. You must recognize the host tree before picking sulfur shelf mushrooms because they are toxic if they grow on some specific trees.

Sulfur shelf mushrooms growing on pine, spruce, juniper, eucalyptus, hemlock, fir, tamarack, or locust trees are poisonous look-alikes. The ones growing on oak trees are the safest. Therefore, if you cannot identify the host tree because it is dead, it is safest not to pick the mushroom.

Moreover, only the young caps of sulfur shelf mushrooms can be cooked and eaten. The stem and the more mature of these mushrooms are too tough to be cooked. The caps of the young ones are popular for their rich and meaty flavor.

The vibrant yellow colors and the impressive size make it very easy to identify the chicken of the wood mushrooms. With a meaty, lemony flavor, the reason for its name is that this mushroom tastes similar to chicken. Some people tend to think that the taste of this mushroom is more aligned with lobster or crab.

Regardless of which meat it tastes similar to, there is no denying that the chicken of the wood mushroom is a delectable substitute for meat, and mushroom eaters love it. Chicken mushrooms can take the place of tofu or chicken in any recipe. One important point of concern is that some people tend to have gastric issues when consuming this mushroom. So, try eating a small amount for the first time, and if you are fine with it, you can go ahead and consume it without fear.

Also, it is important to remember NOT to pick chicken mushrooms growing on eucalyptus, cedar, or coniferous trees. These are known to contain toxins that could create problems for some people. Here are some basic facts about chicken of the wood mushrooms before we move into a more detailed understanding of identifying characteristics:

- There are many species of chicken of the woods mushrooms. They can be saprophytic or parasitic fungi. You are most likely to find them at the base of a living or a dead tree.
- They have a distinctive yellowish-orange color that makes it very easy to identify them. They normally grow in large clusters of overlapping brackets. The yellowish-orange color fades as the mushrooms mature.

- Other chicken names of the wood are sulfur shelf, chicken fungus, and chicken mushroom. They belong to the genus Laetiporus.

- There are currently about 12 different species of chicken mushrooms. Some of them include Laetiporus sulphureus, Laetiporus Cincinnatus (both found on Eastern North America), Laetiporus gilbertsonii (found on the west coast of North America), and Laetiporus conifericola (found in Western North America).

Considered a 'safe' mushroom for beginners, chickens can be easily identified with the following characteristic features:

- This mushroom does not have a stem, and therefore, there is no height to talk about.

- The caps themselves grow into large-sized brackets ranging from 2 to 10 inches in diameter and up to 10 inches in length.

- The fan-shaped brackets can be smooth or slightly wrinkled. The brackets grow in an overlapping pattern and appear stacked on top of each other. Therefore, the entire fruiting body can become quite large.

- Both the outside and the inside of the cap are yellowish-orange in color. With age, the brightness of the flesh, as well as the colors of the exterior, fades. Also, mature chicken mushrooms tend to have hard and crumbly flesh.

- There are no gills under the caps, only yellowish or whitish pores from which the spores are dispersed. As the caps are clustered together and not distinct, it is not easy to get spores of chicken mushrooms.

Chicken mushrooms always grow at or on the base of living or dead trees. They never grow out directly from the soil or the ground. Mostly, they grow on dying or dead hardwoods, especially oak, although you can find them at the base of beech and cherry trees as well. Chickens growing on cedar and eucalyptus should be avoided as they can cause gastric distress.

They can be harvested from summer right through fall, which means you will find many chickens mushrooming between August and October. In warmer climates, you can find them even in the early winter months too. Some general cooking tips for chicken mushrooms:

Young specimens work best in your dishes as these mushrooms become harder and brittle as they age. Look for tender and juicy caps that ooze a liquid when you cut them. Also, the margins of the brackets are better for cooking than the centers, which have a woody or corky flavor, which is not necessarily pleasant to eat. Because they are so spongy and light, it is best to clean them with a damp cloth as regular washing might result in water-logging them.

They can be refrigerated in a paper bag for not more than a week. Cut them into small, bite-sized pieces before cooking them. You can blanch, fry, sauté, or bake them. You can preserve them by sautéing and freezing them for later use. Another important point to remember is to be careful with the amount of oil you use while cooking chickens. They tend to absorb a lot of oil, giving you stomach issues later on.

Pasta Sauce with Chicken of the Woods Mushrooms

Ingredients:

- Butter - 4 tbsps
- Young chicken mushrooms (cleaned and chopped finely) - 1 pound
- Shallots (finely chopped) - 1
- Sherry or dry white wine - ¼ cup
- Milk - 1 cup
- Vegetable stock - 1 cup
- Flour - 3 tbsp
- Dried or fresh sprigs of thyme
- Salt and pepper

Directions:

1. Melt the butter in a pan and cook the shallots and mushrooms, stirring continuously. First, the mushroom will release their liquids, and then they will reabsorb it. This process will take about 10 minutes.

2. Next, add the wine and cook for another 5-10 minutes. Mix the stock and milk, bring to a boil, and then simmer slowly.

3. In another pot, melt the remaining butter. Stir in the flour slowly and cook for about 4 minutes. Remove from the heat and whisk in the simmering stock/milk mixture, taking a little amount at a time. Adding the entire liquid will create a big messy clump.

4. Add the thyme to this sauce and put it back on the stove to cook for another 4-5 minutes while stirring vigorously to prevent lumping. Now, mix in the mushrooms and season with salt and pepper. This sauce can be served with any pasta of your choice. If you use this sauce, you may not need too much cheese in your pasta dish.

Reishi Mushrooms

Reishi mushrooms are one of the best and easiest mushrooms for a beginner forager to start his or her foraging journey. They are easy to identify and do not have any toxic look-alikes making them relatively safe for picking and consumption. Reishi mushrooms are a bit tough to eat. But, their medicinal values are excellently backed by plenty of scientific research. Other names including: also know reishi mushrooms

- Lingzhi
- Mushroom of immortality
- Herb of spiritual potency
- 10000-year mushroom
- Artists' conk
- Varnish self

Many varieties of Reishi mushrooms exist all around the globe, although their medicinal benefits and properties are more or less the same, regardless of their geography. All the species grow on dead and dying trees. These fungi fruit annually (harvest season is in summer), and like many other species, once you find them on any dead and decaying stump of a dying tree, you can keep coming back to that location each year during the harvest season and find new fruiting bodies growing there. This will continue until all the nutrients from the stump are used up by the mycelium.

Identifying characteristics of Reishi mushrooms are:

- They are a fan- or kidney-shaped and have a distinctive color ranging between red and orange.
- The top of the mushroom has a lacquered, shiny finish.
- There are no gills, and the underside of the cap is white when young, which gets gray or tan as the mushrooms mature. The underside of the cap also has tiny pink dots resembling pinpricks.

- Reishi mushrooms grow horizontally out of the wood stump or log.
- The stems are either very short or completely absent.
- Reishi mushrooms have a strong woody, though pleasant smell. Some people think the smell is similar to decomposing leaf mulch.
- Spores come out from the underside of the caps. The spore print of Reishi mushrooms is brown. You can also find spores on the logs and the caps of the lower mushrooms as the spores from the upper ones fall on them. The sprinkling of spores from the upper mushrooms tends to dull the red-orange color of the caps.
- The flesh of the mushroom becomes tan or brown when bruised. The characteristic red-orange cap of the hemlock Reishi variety is visible as it matures.
- Commonly, Reishi mushrooms are 4 to 6 inches in width and about 0.5 to 1 inch in thickness. However, some can

grow to about 2 inches in thickness and up to a foot in width.

- Most Reishi mushrooms do not last for more than a few days because slugs begin to devour them as they mature.

It is important to harvest only those mushrooms whose cap's underside is white. Molds tend to grow on the tanned/browned and mature Reishi mushrooms. Also, as these mushrooms can bruise rapidly after harvesting, preserving them quickly is important. You can easily identify the new and young white mushrooms as they emerge from the mycelium.

There are multiple species of Reishi mushrooms and the ones found in North America are:

Ganoderma lucidum is a common ingredient in Chinese medicine and grows in warmer climates such as Asia, southern Europe, and the South Pacific. In North America, you can find this species of Reishi mushrooms in the Southeastern US.

Ganoderma Curtisii - This species of Reishi mushrooms can be found from Massachusetts up to Nebraska. With a distinctive ochre-colored cap, this species has a matte rather than a shiny lacquer finish on top. Mostly, it is found on maple and oak logs. But these mushrooms also grow on other hardwoods.

Ganoderma Tsugae - This species is commonly referred to as hemlock Reishi or sometimes as hemlock varnish shelf. Tsugae means hemlock, which indicates where these mushrooms commonly grow. Although hemlock trees are typical hosts for this species of Reishi mushrooms, you can also find them on birch or maple trees, especially those that are close to hemlock trees. You will find the freshest hemlock Reishi mushrooms between May and July.

As mentioned earlier, there are no toxic look-alikes of Reishi mushrooms, making them one of the ideal mushrooms for novice foragers. It can, however, be quite a difficult task to distinguish between the various species of Reishi mushrooms. However, all of them are cooked and preserved in the same way. Also, the nutritional benefits of all the species are the same. The subtle differences between the species are more for academics than mushroom consumers.

To reiterate a point mentioned earlier, pick only young Reishi mushrooms with white undersides and bright caps. The older mushrooms with dull caps and brownish or tanned undersides tend to have a lot of potentially harmful molds and should not be eaten.

You can either pull the mushroom gently from the host tree or use a knife to cut the softer specimens. Also, you must make sure you are not picking mushrooms growing around other toxic plants, trees, and vegetation, especially poison ivy, which can sometimes be found close by.

A word of caution about consuming Reishi for people on other medications, especially for the liver: there are records of allergic reactions when combined with Reishi and certain liver medications. But, the reactions stopped immediately after Reishi was discontinued.

They have to be quickly dried because they spoil rapidly. Dried Reishi mushrooms should be stored in airtight containers away from direct sunlight. You can also make a mushroom tincture with Reishi mushrooms immediately after harvesting them. They have both alcohol-soluble and water-soluble constituents in them. Therefore, a double extraction method of tincture preparation will ensure you get optimal medicinal benefits from this wonderful species.

As a medicine, the best way to consume Reishi mushrooms is to make a strong tea with thinly sliced mushrooms simmered for about 1-2 hours in water. The dried mushrooms can be powdered and used in other dishes or put into Reishi capsules and taken daily to boost your immunity.

1. Reishi Mushroom Vegetable Soup

Ingredients:

- Olive oil - 1 tbsp
- Onion (diced) - 1
- Garlic cloves (minced) - 4
- Peeled and grated fresh ginger - 2 tbsp
- Carrots (sliced) - 2
- Fennel bulb (diced) - 1
- A mixture of wild mushrooms (sliced) - 4 cups
- Water - 6 cups
- Reishi mushroom powder - ¼ cup
- Miso paste - ¼ cup
- Allspice - 1 tbsp
- Fresh thyme - 1 tbsp
- Kale (chopped) - 3 cups
- Salt and pepper - to taste

Directions:

Heat oil in a large pot and add onions to the heated oil. Sauté for 2 minutes. Then add garlic and sauté for another minute. Then add the ginger and all the other chopped veggies. Reishi powder should not be added at this time. Sauté this mixture for 5 minutes.

Now, add the water, dry spices, miso paste, and Reishi powder. Bring the liquid mixture to a boil. Reduce the flame to a simmer and cook the broth for about an hour. Lastly, add the kale into the hot broth to wilt. Add the required salt and pepper, and your Reishi mushroom vegetable soup is ready.

Hedgehog

Hydnum repandum is the scientific name of the hedgehog mushroom. Identifying these mushrooms is quite easy, and they are absolutely delicious. Apart from that, hedgehog mushrooms are extremely nutritious. They are rich in protein, low in calories, and low in fat. They contain helpful minerals such as zinc, calcium, magnesium, manganese, and iron.

These mushrooms have a misshapen cap that is orange in color and are usually several inches wide. The underside of the mushroom usually has downward-pointing spines similar to those of a hedgehog and hence its name. This misshapen cap rests on a visible stalk that's orange. They tend to bloom from mid-fall until late summer. If you find them in a specific spot one year, chances are you will find them in the same spot the following year too. These delicious mushrooms work perfectly well with several Italian and French dishes.

White MatsutakeMushroom

White Matsutake/Pine Mushroom (Tricholoma magnivelare)

Edibility: Scrumptious and highly coveted owing to its unique flavor. The white matsutake is said to taste like autumn, with hints of cypress and sweet cinnamon and a slightly spicy kick. Some cooks like to make the most of this spicy blend by marinating it for around ten minutes in dry sherry, soy sauce, and neutral oil, then roasting it until it takes on a golden-brown color. Others feel that this mushroom is best served simply, grilled or infused into broths or paired with rice or butter. Matsutake mushrooms lend a unique flavor to various dishes ranging from stews to chicken and fish dishes. Even when you freeze them for a few months, they retain their wonderful flavor.

Habitat: Coniferous forests, where they generally grow from September to November.

Physical Description: The cap of this popular mushroom (5 to 20 cm in diameter) is white as it first emerges from the duff though it eventually tans a little and develops reddish-brown scales. It also changes its shape from convex to flat as it matures. Its gills are attached and close together, and they change from a creamy to a tan hue as they mature. The stipe (4 to 15 cm in length and 2 to 6 cm wide) is cream-hued with a white veil that breaks irregularly, leaving red/brown scales beneath the ring. The mushroom can be swollen near the base then develop a pointy base that can be found deep within the soil.

Spore Print: White and subglobular (almost globe-shaped) with an apicular point.

Lookalikes: *Amanita smithiana*, which is poisonous. Don't simply rely on smell to differentiate between these mushrooms because *smithianas* can smell quite similar. There are a few tests that foragers use to determine if they have, indeed, found a delicious matsutake. Remember that they have a very firm stem that is very difficult to separate from the cap and gills. Another test involves placing the mushroom in the palm of your hand and squeezing down hard on the stem. If you push hard enough, the *Amanita* stem will break. Finally, take a look at the shape of the end of the stem. *Amanitas* have a torpedo-shaped base (similar to a parsnip) that is located beneath the ground. On the other hand, Matsutakes do not burrow deep into the soil and are widest above the soil near the ring. Finally, you can try an overnight test that involves leaving the mushrooms in a pile overnight. *Amanitas* have geotropic stipes and bend to reorient their gills, while matsutake stems remain straight. If in doubt, simply throw the mushroom out, as one meal simply isn't worth a few days in a hospital.

Fun Fact 1: This mushroom can be harder to find because it "hides" in the ground. Be on the lookout for a little hump on the forest floor. You could get lucky and find many more if you find one since they are sometimes found in circles or lines. Sometimes they only come out of the ground fully when they are mature, so be on the lookout for something that looks like a half-buried golf ball during your foraging adventures. When you forage them, take note of their unique smell, described as a blend of cinnamon and sweaty socks.

Fun Fact 2: Matsutakes are highly prized around the world. In Japan, *Armillaria matsutakes* cost up to $250 per kilogram, and this species is very similar to the American variety. Because white matsutakes are so coveted, foragers can only collect up to six of them for incidental and non-commercial use in the Siuslaw National Forest.

Fun Fact 3: When foraging for matsutakes, you could have an unexpected competitor: deer! They love this mushroom, which, sadly, human beings have not cultivated successfully.

Morels Mushroom

Morel mushrooms are found abundantly across North America, especially the United States growing under hardwood trees. The harvest season for morels consists of a very short window during springtime. This harvest window varies from place to place. Distinctive features of morel mushrooms include:

The yellowish-gray and deeply wrinkled 'honeycombed' cap, which is hollow through the center. This mushroom is typically 2

to 9 cm in height and 2 to 5 cm in thickness. Some poisonous varieties have honeycombed caps like the edible morels. When in doubt, keep them in a separate container to check with experts later on, or don't pick them at all.

Morels have a very strong taste and are delicious when cooked with butter. Morels with leeks are a favorite combination for many mushroom lovers.

You have to pay attention to many questions while looking for morel mushrooms. Questions such as when to look, where to look, what they look like, what looks like them, and more.

When to look: It is important to know that the best time to harvest morel mushrooms is springtime. Black morels are the first ones to arrive, and they are followed by yellow morels about three weeks later. Morels have also been spotted during winter. They have a mind of their own when it comes to when they want to grow.

Where to look: Morel mushrooms occupy the temperate zones of both hemispheres. Unlike some mushrooms, morels do not grow on trees. They do not grow on wood. You will always find them on the ground, growing in groups or clusters. Sometimes they are scattered, and some are even found to grow all alone. If you come across one morel, stop and look around. Chances are you will find many more within the vicinity. Take a look around areas that are covered by the tree shadows, and you are bound to come across a cluster or two.

It is easier to locate the morels mushrooms if you know which tree they ground around. Most morels are associated with the tree around which they grow.

Since black morels are the first ones to appear during the morel season, we will talk about them first. They generally grow around coniferous trees and are mostly found in north-western America. Areas with human activity are also favorable for the growth of morel mushrooms. Black morels are also found near ash, so visiting burnt areas would make finding morels very easy.

Yellow morels are more common in eastern North America and the Midwestern countries. They grow around hardwood trees, including tulips, ash, poplar, and dead or dying elm trees. They also grow in old apple orchards.

These are just general places where you might find what you are looking for. There are instances where yellow morels grow around coniferous trees, and black morels grow around hardwood trees.

Study shows that morels love to grow in alkaline soils. This explains their preference for apple orchards and burnt areas. Forest fires create ash, which boosts the alkalinity of the surrounding soil. Apple trees also favor alkaline soils for growth. So before planting apple trees, the soil is treated with calcium carbonate, which is called liming. The new, treated, alkaline soil proves to be a favorable condition for the growth of morels.

What they look like: many species of mushrooms can be categorized into black and yellow morels. Morels take on a conical shape. They are long and lean mushrooms, unlike most common mushrooms, short and wide. Morels take on a variety of colors.

The caps have characteristic dull colors like yellow-brown, gray, grayish-black, olive, etc., while the stalk takes on a whitish color. The caps of morel mushrooms are very different from other mushrooms. Once you know what to look for, it will be hard to misidentify a morel mushroom.

Their caps are ridged on the outside, and they have a honeycomb-like appearance inside. Their caps are also fully attached to the stalk. It seems as if the caps emerge from the stalk and meet at the top. When we cut open a morel mushroom lengthwise, we can see that it is filled with a cottony substance.

What looks like them: There are many toxic look-alikes of morels, and it is important to learn to discern between them so that you don't end up consuming the wrong ones. Yet, the differences between them are not very difficult to learn and master, although as a novice, you must take second opinions in case of doubt (keep them in a separate basket to ask an expert later on, or someone in your group can help too), or better still, don't pick them up until you are absolutely sure.

- **Half-free morels**: this mushroom isn't exactly a look-alike of a morel mushroom except for the fact that it has a white stalk. The caps of the half-free morels are short. Moreover, when we cut open this mushroom lengthwise, we can see that the cap does not originate fully from the stalk, rather it is only half attached to the stalk. Hence the name half-free morels.

- **Wrinkled thimble-cap**: as the name suggests, this mushroom has a very wrinkled cap, unlike a morel mushroom, which has a ridged cap. These mushrooms are very short. Their cap is attached to the tip of the stalk and spreads in all directions from the tip like an umbrella. The sides of the cap hang freely.

- **False morels**: the differences between false and true morels are as clear as night and day. False morels are short mushrooms with a wrinkled, dark reddish colored cap. Their stock is very wide as well. When you cut lengthwise, false morels appear folded on the inside, whereas true morels appear hollow with a cottony filling. It is important to differentiate between false and true morels. Some species of false morels like G.esculenta, on consumption, can lead to problems including nausea, fever and fatigue, liver and kidney failure, and sometimes even death.

How to consume: Black and yellow morels are one of the most favored edible mushrooms. But just like all wild mushrooms, it is never meant to be eaten raw. Morels taste best when cooked in butter or oil.

Cooking Morels

We have talked to a lot of people about cooking morels, and the most common question is how to tell when the morels are fully cooked. Do not undercook morels, as mushrooms are not easily digestible. Fully cooking them brings out the full flavor, kills any bacteria, and makes them more digestible. When sautéing morels, the morels are done when the mushrooms make a popping sound, like bacon when it's crisping. When deep-frying morels with a batter, the morels will float to the top when the batter is done; the morel itself is done when the fried mushroom shakes and then releases bubbles. The bubbles are the indicator.

The first time you eat any wild mushroom, try a small sample. If you don't react (flulike symptoms) within twenty-four hours, eat on. We eat morels throughout the year, and our bodies are used to them. We usually eat small amounts as condiments or appetizers to our meal. When fresh mushrooms are available, you might be tempted to cook a big batch and eat them all, but it's better to start the season with small batches, like appetizers, working up to larger amounts (like the main meal) toward the end of the season.

Morels, like all mushrooms, cook more evenly when you cut and separate the caps and stems. Caps and stems have different textures and cook differently. Stems take a minute or two longer to cook than caps. Cutting the morels into ringlets allows you to cook the inside and the outside of the morel evenly with full contact with the skillet. When you sauté morels in butter or oil, they first become very soupy as the moisture cooks out of the mushrooms. Further along in the cooking process, the moisture diminishes and the morels begin to make a popping sound. If you are using real butter the butter will be clarified at this point.

Separate caps and stems for cooking.

When batter frying morels, it is much harder to hear the popping sound over the oil itself popping, so be sure to allow the morels plenty of time to cook. When the batter is cooked, the morels will float to the top. The fried mushrooms will shake and release bubbles when they are fully cooked.

Most people eat their morels sautéed, fried, or deep-fried. But if you're adding them to a recipe, morels should be precooked. Each of the basic recipes that follow can be varied to suit your family.

Sautéed Morels

Clean the morels, pat them dry, and cut them into ringlets of equal size. Separate the caps from the stems.

Add 2-3 tablespoons of butter and 1-2 tablespoons of extra virgin olive oil to a skillet on medium-high heat. Canola oil, peanut oil, and grape seed oil all work well too. The oil helps keep the butter from burning.

Add a small amount of granulated or chopped fresh garlic. Mushrooms take on the flavors of whatever they are cooked with. Go light on the seasonings, and add salt and pepper when the mushrooms come out of the skillet.

Ringlets.

Fill the bottom of the pan with morels, starting with the stems and then the caps a minute or two later. Stir gently. Don't crowd the skillet—you may need to cook them in separate batches. The morels will first become soupy, but the liquid will evaporate as they cook. When the butter is clarified and the mushrooms make a popping noise similar to bacon sizzling, they are done. Serve warm with the clarified butter. They are best served with a light cracker and strong cheese like aged New York or Wisconsin cheddar. Match with a semisweet fruity wine.

Use flavored oil, such as sesame oil, to alter the flavor of the morels. A touch of soy sauce gives them a slight Asian saltiness. Use a variety of herbs based on your tastes. Start out with a light touch. Morels absorb the flavors they are cooked with.

One of the joys of finding a lot of morels is preserving them and experimenting with flavors based on the season. Sautéed morels are good over venison and domestic roasts and can be used as the base for cream of morel soup.

Morels and Bacon

This works with all varieties of morels. When we find a lot of half-cap morels, this is what we do with all of them. Render bacon with half-caps to make a sauce for roasts, wild game, rice or pasta dishes, or eggs. For a gourmet grilled cheese sandwich put a few tablespoons of this recipe between the cheese slices.

Use a quarter pound of bacon (or ham) for each pound of morels. Cut the bacon into small pieces. Fry the bacon until crisp. The bacon must be cooked to the desired crispness before adding the morels. Add prepared morels cut into ringlets—first the stems and the caps a minute or so later. If you are using half-cap morels, the stems do not need to be cooked separately from the caps. The liquid will become clear as it cooks, and the morels will make a popping sound. Remove immediately from the heat. Drain off any excess liquid (it can be saved and used to season meat). We prefer to use hickory smoked ham or bacon; the bacon produces a saltier version of the recipe. If you are combining this with another recipe, save the drained liquid and substitute it for part of the liquid or fat of the dish.

RICE PILAF WITH MORELS

- 1 lb. morels

- ¼ lb. bacon or 3 T. butter and 1 T. oil

- 2 cups uncooked long-grain rice

- ⅓ cup chopped green onions

- 3½ cups water

- Salt and pepper to taste

Prepare either basic sautéed morels or bacon and morels in a large skillet. When fully cooked, add two cups of uncooked rice. Let it sizzle until most of the rice pops. Add chopped green onions and water. Cover and steam for about twenty minutes, or until the water has been absorbed. Serve with game meat, pheasant, or any kind of roast.

Button Mushrooms

Botanical Name: Agaricus bisporus

This mushroom also has the names white mushrooms or baby mushrooms. You are sure to find these because they are the most common variety of mushrooms available. They are small to medium in size. The size of their caps ranges between 5-7 cm. Sort truncated caps remain attached to the caps. The spongy and white caps are firm and rounded. When you bruise them, the white flesh will change color to pink and then brown.

There are small light brown gills on the underside of the white caps. They remain under a white veil. We get dark brown spores from these gills, and the stems are also edible, thick, smooth, and dense. Before cooking, they have a mild but crisp texture. They display their typical earthy flavor with a chewy and tender texture when cooked.

You can get the white mushrooms allaround the year. The botanical classification for this is Agaricus bisporus. It is one of the most cultivated varieties and is well used in this family. Sometimes people refer to it as Table Mushrooms, Cultivated Mushrooms, Champignon de Paris, and Common Mushrooms. They are recognizable by their color and age, but they closely resemble the larger portobello mushroom or, the smaller cremini mushroom. Age-wise, button mushrooms are the youngest, after which come the cremini mushrooms, and then we have the portobello mushrooms. White button mushrooms grow in grasslands and fields in many places the world over. People also cultivate them, and the varieties in this group account for 90% of all cultivated mushroom varieties. Home cooks and chefs prefer them for their versatility and mild taste.

Nutritional Value

Along with antioxidants, white button mushrooms contain selenium, potassium, manganese, folate, zinc, phosphorus, riboflavin, vitamin D, and amino acids.

Applications

We use white mushrooms, both cooked and raw, while stewing, grilling, sautéing, roasting, and baking. In many instances, we use them instead of cremini mushrooms when the latter is not available. Sliced raw, the button mushrooms get combined with grain and green salad.

Cooked, we stuff them with crabs and grill them on skewers along with cheese and meat. They serve as a good appetizer or a baked tart. We add them to sauces, stews, soups, and stir-fries. They also combine well with artichokes. We can bake them into mushroom bread or chop them into ceviche.

They pair well with carrots, tomatoes, celery, basil, parsley, sage, lime, kimchi, fennel, ginger, onion, shallots, jalapenos, and potatoes. We use them along with meats like pork, beef, egg, or poultry. They combine with cream sauce, marinara sauce, balsamic vinegar, white wine, soy sauce, pecorino Romano, parmesan, mozzarella cheese, orzo, and rice.

It is possible to store them in the fridge for up to a week. Cover them up with moist paper towels to prolong their life.

Cultural Beliefs and Ethnic Values

People have used this variety of mushrooms since ancient times. So, they have a variety of uses and symbolism in different cultures. In Egypt, people believed that eating mushrooms will give them the secret power to eternal life. They cultivated the white mushrooms beneath the catacombs in Paris (hence the name Champignon de Paris). The Chinese used them to regulate the energy in the body and promote well-being.

Cremini Mushrooms

This variety of mushrooms (also called crimini mushrooms) belongs to the same as button mushrooms. But they have a deeper flavor and a little brown color. All varieties of mushrooms were brown until 1926, when a Pennsylvanian farmer discovered a batch of white mushrooms. He began to sell them as a separate variety from then on.

The button and portobello mushrooms also belong to the cremini mushroom group. Where they differ is in how long they mature. White mushrooms are the youngest, and people grow them for their white color and soft texture. The cremini mushrooms that we are discussing here come between white and portobello mushrooms. We allow them to ripen a little more than the button mushrooms. This gives them a little stronger taste, but they remain like white mushrooms. Some people refer to them as baby portobello mushrooms.

When they age past the first two stages, they become portobello mushrooms. That is, they are mature mushrooms. They have a larger size, and the gills underneath the caps are denser. Cremini is the preferred variety for many people because they are "right" for their taste buds.

Identify this Variety

They have a little brownish appearance, but the stems are whitish. These mushrooms are more textured and shaggier than the white mushrooms. The gills are completely sheathed, and if you cut them across, they will be completely white, with the beginnings of the gills visible.

It isn't advisable to forage for these mushrooms on your own. You will get Agaricus bisporus and their cousin Agaricus campestris, the field mushroom. To those unfamiliar with mushrooms, the Agaricus campestris will look the same as amanita specimens.

Aminta poisoning will not manifest up to five hours after eating them. It might even take a full day for the poisoning to show symptoms. If one delays it, the poison will have damaged the liver and kidneys. Since this variety of mushrooms is available in plenty in the malls, you don't need to try foraging and risk getting poisoned.

Growing the Mushroom

It is easy to grow since mushrooms don't require light (they have no chlorophyll). Take compost to begin. Use any medium - straw, dry poultry waste, canola meal, water, or gypsum - and pasteurize the compost so that all fungal spores and bacteria already present get destroyed. Take concentrated mycelium culture and colonize it for several weeks. Mix this cremini spawn evenly in the compost.

Wait for a few days until the mycelium colonizes the compost. Add a layer of peat moss to give more moisture to the growing mushrooms. It will take 2-3 weeks for the mushroom to appear. You can also introduce mushrooms to shorten the waiting time. Once they appear, they grow very fast; they double in size once a day! They reach the cremini stage in about four days and are ready for picking.

Picking the cremini mushrooms is a handoperation. Cut cleanly at the stem with a knife. Avoid touching it many times, as this will increase the chances of bruising them. It is advisable to wait until it is time to cook them and harvest them. Cremini mushrooms are great because of their strong, earthy taste. To make soups, sauté them a little as they will taste better this way than raw.

Be sure to wash them before cooking since there might be a little dirt on them even if they come pre-washed. If you are not cooking them immediately, store them in the refrigerator instantly after buying them. It will keep for about a week, so make sure you cook them before then. Freezing is not recommended, as this will alter its texture and taste. A good option is to sauté the mushrooms and cool them. Then, place them in airtight bags and put them in the freezer.

Also, do not pile up other foodstuffs on top of the mushroom. If you bruise them, they will spoil. Don't keep them next to food with strong odors like fish. The mushroom absorbs flavors, and so they will taste different. And, don't put them in the vegetable tray. There is far too much moisture there for the mushrooms to survive.

Whether you should eat raw mushrooms, many serve them along with vegetables as a salad.

Portobello Mushrooms

This is the grown version of the button mushroom. They are much larger than the white and cremini mushrooms. They have a meatier texture, but the flavor is still mild. Their caps are open, and you can see the dark gills beneath. Due to the big size, people use portobellos to make burgers. They stuff them with ingredients and bake them instead of frying them.

The portobello (also portabella) mushrooms are popular and delicious. People thought they were a separate species until recent research showed that they were only mature creminis.

Caution: Never eat portobellos raw; they contain hydrazine and agaritine. These are toxic substances.

Portabellas are the most common mushrooms used in burgers and pizzas. They can grow in any environment and all year-round. People didn't know about them until 1980, when they changed their name. This is the largest consumed mushroom in the world.

Health Benefits

Anti-cancer properties - There are many ingredients in portobellos, such as grifolin, beta-glucans, lectins, and lentinan, that inhibit the growth of cancer cells. More specifically, CLA, a phytochemical, inhibits cell proliferation. It induces apoptosis (make the cells cause suicide) in cancer cells and help in lipid metabolism. According to a study conducted in mice, Portobello mushrooms cause a reduction in the size of tumors. Another study showed how the beta-glucans were responsible for the death of cancer cells.

Good for the Blood - portobello mushrooms contain large amounts of copper and selenium. The human body uses copper to form hemoglobin, and red blood cells are useful for our respiration. It also helps in tissue repair and improves our metabolism. This helps prevent fatigue and produces energy by breaking down oxygen. Selenium helps enhance thyroid function, which helps us avoid hyperthyroidism. It also helps us overcome anxiety and depression by improving hormone activity.

Useful anti-inflammatory property - The antioxidants help control inflammation. It has fibers and L-ergothioneine that help fight inflammations in the body.

Cooking mushrooms will make them safe and more palatable though they will shrink in volume. Portobellos are good for roasting. When you cook them, the agaritine in them, being heat unstable, will disintegrate.

Oyster Mushroom

One of the favorites of mushroom lovers, the Pleurotus ostreatus mushroom, grows in tropical and temperate forests on dead and decaying wooden logs in shelf-like clusters. It has the name dhingri (Hindi), pearl oyster mushroom, and tree oyster mushroom. It belongs to the Pleurotus family and is a basidiomycete. It has an aroma of bitter almonds.

Parts of the Oyster Mushroom

There are three significant parts to the oyster mushroom.

a. Fleshy shell - a cap shaped like a spatula (pileus).

b. Stalk - short or long, central, or lateral (stipe).

c. Gills - underneath the pileus (lamellae).

This mushroom has a relatively large size, and gills are whitish. The stem is almost absent. In North America, it begins to sprout in October and goes on until early April. The kind of wood it grows on and the season it grows help separate one species from the next.

To Preserve the Environment

They kill bacteria and nematodes to such a large extent that conservationists use these mushrooms to clean environmental wastes. But the extent of the effort is not enough to clean the planet (through mycoremediation) or clean water (through mycofiltration).

Description of the Parts

Caps: The caps are 3-15 cm across with a broad, convex shape. They become flat to the top with a fan-shaped or kidney-shaped outline. They are bald with a greasy feel when they are wet or fresh. This is a sign of edible mushrooms. Color is pale to dark brown and fading slowly, and margins are a little enrolled in young mushrooms.

Stem: Lateral and rudimentary and almost absent when growing on trees, the stems are present when growing on logs. They grow up to 7 cm in length and 3 cm across with a tough, hairy, and velvety texture.

Gills: Run down to the stem, short and whitish to gray, becoming yellow with time. They have brownish edges and have black beetles growing inside.

The odor is distinct but hard to classify, and the flesh is white and thick. It doesn't change when we slice it. Spores are cylindric, ellipsoid, and 7-11 ??m x 2-4 ??m.

Habitat

This grows freely in the temperate and tropical regions of the world. But it is absent in the Pacific Northwest region where some other species grow. It grows allaround the year in the UK.

Cooking and Dishes

Korean, Chinese, and Japanese cuisine uses the oyster mushroom or other vegetables and ingredients to make soups and other culinary delicacies. It is good to eat on its own, as a soup, or as a stuffed dish. One must use the young mushroom when it is soft because they become as tough as they age. The taste is mild, and its odor resembles that of anise. While cooking, the mushrooms get torn up instead of getting sliced because this gives a better flavor.

Oyster dishes are popular in Kerala, the coastal town of India. They cultivate it in clear polythene bags that they layer with buns of hay. Now, they sow the spawn between the layers. Czech and Slovak cuisine also sees the use of Oyster mushrooms where they eat it with or instead of meat.

Pearl oyster is useful to those who make mycelium furniture and mycelium bricks.

Warning: The sugar alcohol Arabitol present in oysters might cause gastrointestinal disturbances in sensitive people.

Mushroom Recipes

Mushroom and Cream Cheese Pizza

Preparation Time: 25 minutes

Yield: 4 **Serves**

So very good! Just like an Italian pizza – simple Ingredients but packed with flavour...

List of Ingredients:

- 2 thin and crispy pizza bases

- 2 tbsp. of olive oil

- 2 garlic cloves – crushed

- 1 cup of button mushrooms – sliced

- 1 cup of Portabella mushrooms – sliced

- 2 spring onions – chopped

- 1 cup of cream cheese

- ½ cup of shredded pizza cheese

- 1 cup of baby rocket

Directions:

- Preheat oven to 410F.
- Place your bases on baking trays.
- In a bowl, mix oil and garlic.
- Spread over bases.

- Top with mushrooms, onion, cream cheese, and pizza cheese.

- Into the oven.

- Bake till golden.

- Place rocket on top and serve up hot – so good!

Mushroom and Tofu Laksa

Preparation Time: 30 minutes

Yield: 4 **Serves**

A beautiful vegetarian meal that anybody would love – full of flavour and goodness...

List of Ingredients:

- 1 packet of rice stick noodles
- 2 cups of shitake mushrooms – sliced thinly
- 2 cups of button mushrooms – sliced thinly
- 2 tbsp. of oil
- 4 cups of Malaysian soup base
- 1 can of coconut milk
- 1 cup of baby snow peas
- 1 packet of silken tofu – cubed
- 1 cup of bean sprouts
- 2 green onions – sliced thinly

Directions:

- Cook your noodles until tender and drain.

- Put to the side.

- Heat oil in a saucepan over a medium flame and cook mushrooms till tender.

- Pour in your soup base and coconut milk.

- Bring to the boil.

- Lower flame and simmer for 4 minutes.

- Add your peas.

- Take off the heat.

- Portion your noodles into bowls.

- Spoon your soup mix over your noodles and serve with sprouts and onion on top.

Mixed Mushroom and Herb Pilaf

Preparation Time: 2 hours and 40 minutes

Yield: 4 **Serves**

This pilaf is a flavoursome light meal packed full of healthy nutrition – team it with a glass of icy white wine...

List of Ingredients:

- 4 cups of mushrooms – sliced
- 1 brown onion – chopped
- 1/3 cup of soy sauce
- 2 tbsp. of honey
- 1 tbsp. of butter
- 2 cups of long grain rice – brown
- 3 cups of vegetable stock
- ½ cup of fresh mixed herbs
- 1 tbsp. of olive oil

Directions:

- In a glass dish, mix soy and honey.
- Add mushrooms and marinate, covered in the fridge for 1 hour.
- Preheat oven to 370F.
- In a saucepan over a medium flame, heat oil and butter and cook onion till tender.
- Add rice and mix well.
- Pour in stock, mushrooms, and marinade.

- Bring to the boil.

- Pour into an ovenproof dish.

- Put the lid on and bake until rice is tender and liquid is reduced.

- Fold through herbs and season.

- Ready to serve.

Mushroom Tart

Preparation Time: 1 hour

Yield: 6 **Serves**

Flaky pastries filled with the flavors of mushrooms

List of Ingredients:

- 1 large sheet of shortcrust pastry
- 2 tbsp. of butter
- 2 red onions – sliced
- 2 cups of button mushrooms – sliced
- 1 cup of Shimeji mushrooms – sliced
- 1 cup of enoki mushrooms – sliced
- 3 garlic cloves – sliced
- 1 tbsp. of thyme leaves
- 2 eggs – free range
- 1 cup of thickened cream
- 1 small packet of brie – sliced

Directions:

- Preheat oven to 380F.
- Grease a flan pan.

- Line with pastry.

- In a large frypan over a high flame, melt butter and cook garlic and onions until tender.

- Cook all mushrooms until tender.

- Add thyme.

- Let it cool.

- In a jug, whisk eggs.

- Season.

- Place mushroom mix into the pastry case.

- Pour egg mixture over the top and top with cheese.

- Into the oven to bake till set and golden.

- Let it stand for 5 minutes out of the oven.

- Serve it up – great for breakfast!!!

Mushroom Zucchini and Bacon Slice

Preparation Time: 1 hour and 15 minutes

Yield: 6 **Serves**

This is a great alternative for the lunch box or a weekend lunch with an added salad – tasty and full of nutrition...

List of Ingredients:

- 2 cups of zucchini – chopped
- 2 cups of button mushrooms – sliced thinly
- 2 cups of bacon – chopped
- 1 onion – chopped
- 1 tbsp. of olive oil
- 1 cup of fresh ricotta
- 7 eggs – free range
- ½ cup of self-rising flour
- ½ tsp. of baking powder
- 1 tbsp. of fresh dill – chopped
- 1 ½ cups of tasty cheese – grated

Directions:

- Preheat oven to 370F.
- Grease a lamington tin.
- Line with baking paper.
- In a non-stick frypan over a medium flame, heat oil and cook onion until tender.
- Add bacon and cook till golden.

- Add mushroom and cook till soft.

- Take off the heat and cool.

- In a large bowl, combine ricotta and eggs.

- Whisk until smooth.

- Keep whisking and add flour.

- Dill, zucchini, bacon and half the cheese get stirred in next.

- Pour into prepared pan.

- Sprinkle remaining cheese over the top.

- Bake until set and golden.

- Serve it up hot or cold.

Mushroom Mozzarella Burgers

Preparation Time: 30 minutes

Yield: 4 **Serves**

This is a delicious burger – pancetta, cheese, and mushrooms – yum!

List of Ingredients:

- 4 large flat mushrooms – stems out

- Olive oil

- 1 brown onion – sliced thinly

- 1 tbsp. of balsamic vinegar

- 4 slices of pancetta

- 8 slices of mozzarella

- 4 crispy rolls

- 1 cup of baby rocket

- 1 tomato – sliced

- Fresh basil leaves

Directions:

- Heat up your barbecue plate and drizzle with oil.

- Cook up your onions until golden.

- Pour a little balsamic on and let the liquid evaporate.

- Place onion in a bowl.

- Oil hot plate again and cook mushrooms until tender.

- Meanwhile, place pancetta onto the hotplate and cook till golden.

- Place mushrooms, stem side up and put 2 slices of cheese on each.

- When cheese has melted, they are ready.

Identifying Poisonous Mushrooms

Not all mushrooms are beneficial for us. Many types of mushrooms are poisonous. Mycetism or mushroom poisoning is the term used when referring to the harmful effects due to the ingestion of the toxins present in mushrooms. And this may range from a simple gastrointestinal discomfort or may even cause death.

One of the most common causes of mushroom poisoning is that people misidentify poisonous ones as edible because of their close resemblance. That is why it is vital for would-be mushroom farmers to be very familiar with the mushrooms they would like to plant and go as far as learning their slight differences with the toxic species that look like them.

Folk traditions have listed certain rules for identifying when a particular mushroom is poisonous or safe. However, even mushroom experts will tell you that there are no generic rules for identifying poisonous mushrooms. Here are some of those folklore rules:

1. Brightly colored mushrooms are poisonous.

2. Animals and insects will naturally avoid toxic mushrooms.

3. Poisonous mushrooms can blacken silver.

4. Poisonous mushrooms normally taste bad.

5. All mushrooms are safe once cooked. (folklore, not to be trusted, always consult an expert)

6. When boiled together with rice, a poisonous mushroom will turn the rice to red.

7. Poisonous mushrooms have a pointed cap.

Things To Know About Mushroom Poisoning:

1. The symptoms of mushroom poisoning may not show immediately. Sometimes, the symptoms can be delayed for up to 12 hours or longer.

2. There are instances when, after ingesting a poisonous mushroom, the symptoms seem to go away. However, the toxin will remain in your system for days.

3. Handling a poisonous mushroom may not be much of a hazard to your health, let's say when taking specimen

samples. However, you can contaminate other mushrooms if you place them all in the same container. When keeping different species of mushrooms, it's best to keep them wrapped separately if you are storing them in the same basket or container, or better yet, just keep them in separate containers.

4. Even edible mushrooms may cause allergic reactions, especially to highly sensitive ones. Make sure to take only a few small bites if it's your first time eating any kind of mushroom.

5. Since most cases of mushroom poisoning among immigrants and foreigners happen due to mistaking a poisonous one with a similarly-looking edible mushroom they have back home, it's best to use local references to identify the mushroom's local species.

6. Mushrooms' common names are sometimes confusing because one mushroom may have up to 4 or 5 other familiar names. Try learning the Latin names for accuracy purposes.

7. Mushroom poisoning has no antidotes. Doctors usually just treat whatever damage the toxins may have done to the body.

Instead of gambling with your safety by following folklore rules, it would be better that we familiarize ourselves with some of the most noted poisonous mushrooms. Here are a couple of samples of poisonous mushrooms:

Amanitas

The Amanita is often mistaken for the edible shaggy mane mushroom or Coprinus comatus, especially when still immature. The Amanita species have been known to cause about 90% of mushroom-related deaths.

The Amanita resembles an egg-shaped button that looks like a small puffball when immature. As it grows, it breaks open and eventually develops into a gilled mushroom with caps that looks like a parasol. The cap may be red, brown, yellow, or white in color. The Amanita also has a cup that looks like a sac at the base of the stem, which is usually buried in the soil, a ring on its stem, a white gill, and a white spore print.

Amanita species naturally grow in woodland grounds and are abundant during the summer and fall seasons. This mushroom is usually found among rotting logs.

Amanitas contain amanitin, which is known to be one of the most lethal poisons found in nature. In fact, ingesting just the mushroom cap can lead to death. It also contains amatoxins, which destroy the liver. Some of the other species belonging to The Amanita are Amanita phalloides or destroying angels, of which the subspecies Amanita virosa, Amanita bisporigera, and Amanita ocreata are part of.

Little Brown Mushrooms

Little brown mushrooms come from the family of capped mushrooms in the phylum Basidiomycota. This mushroom category comprises hundreds of different species ranging from small to medium-sized mushrooms. They also come in various colors, from brown to tan, with the cap and well-defined stalk that most mushrooms have. Even mushroom experts are having difficulty sorting little brown mushrooms into species, of which most are poisonous.

Little brown mushrooms thrive in summer, spring, and fall in almost any kind of habitat. They grow well on wood, soil, lawns, forests, and pasture lands. Some little brown mushrooms are harmless, but because they come in such a wide variety, it would be best to avoid all of them. Some mushroom species are mildly poisonous, some hallucinogenic, and still others lethal.

Big Laughing Jim

Big Laughing Jim is from the family Cortinariaceae. This mushroom is described as a big orange-yellow mushroom with a ring on its stalk. It also grows in clusters among trunks and tree stumps from August to October. This mushroom usually grows as a mycelium network on rotting logs and tree roots. Its cap usually ranges in color from orange to fawn. It also has tiny smooth scales. Its gills and spore print are normally yellow or rust, and the gills' spacing is rather crowded. It smells similar to anise and has a bitter taste.

Big Laughing Jim looks similar to the Honey Mushroom or Armillaria mellea and the Ringless Honey Mushroom or the Armillaria tabescens. It has also been compared to that of the Jack-o'lantern (Omphalotus illudens) and the deadly Galeria (Galerina autumnalis). \

Big Laughing Jim species are poisonous. Though some stories circulate that there are instances of experiencing only mild hallucinogenic effects, that occur very rarely happens.

Big Red False Morel

Big Red False Morel (Gyromitra caroliniana) is from the family Discinaceae. It's a reddish-brown brain-like cap that has a white stalk with cottony tissue. It is similar to Gabled false morel (Gyromitra brunnea) and true morels (Morchella spp.)

The Big Red False Morel is usually around from March to May. It grows in groups in mixed woods. Its cap grows from 1 ½ to 7 inches and can grow to about 10 inches in height. This mushroom is potentially deadly. Although some people from Missouri who accidentally ate false morels did not have any ill effects afterward, some people have suffered serious illnesses and died.

Deadly Galerina

Deadly galerina comes from the family Hymenogastraceae. This mushroom has a sticky brown cap, a gill that ranges from yellow to rush, and a ring on its stalk. Some of the mushrooms that look similar to deadly galerina are velvet foot (Flammulina velutipes), honey mushroom (Armillaria mellea), and ringless honey mushroom.

Deadly galerina grows along with coniferous logs and often is scattered or clustered. It is abundant all year round, especially during the months of September to November.

This mushroom contains amatoxins, which is naturally accumulated in the liver cells. Amatoxins disrupt the function of the liver. It also attacks the kidneys. Once ingested, amatoxins may result in severe abdominal pain, diarrhea, and vomiting lasting from six to nine hours. More severe effects may affect the liver and result in gastrointestinal bleeding and even coma. Some have been known to suffer from kidney failure and even death within seven days of consumption.

Destroying Angel

Destroying Angel is a group of closely related deadly all-white mushrooms from the genus Amanita. It comes from the family Amanitaceae. Aside from being an all-white mushroom, it is also noted for its ring on its stalk. It also has a large sac-like cup around its base. Destroying angels are naturally found in the woods and grasses, usually near trees. They are abundant during the months of June to November.

Its cap has a central swelling and a smooth margin which is shiny white, and it gets tacky when wet. Its gills are narrow to broad and have a close spacing. Its stalk is sometimes enlarged at the base and has a cottony texture. Its spores, when magnified, are smooth and are almost round to round. Destroying angels are often mistaken for meadow mushrooms except for the latter's gills, which turn brown.

Destroying Angel is a deserving name because of its toxicity level. Some symptoms of destroying angel poisoning are vomiting, cramps, and diarrhea which appear 6-24 hours after ingestion. It hits the kidney and liver and may eventually cause death. Even livestock and pets are not exempt from this mushroom's toxin.

Emetic Russula

Emetic Russula, also called Russula emetic, is sometimes referred to as "the sickener." It is a basidiomycete mushroom. It comes from the family Russulaceae. It has a red cap that has off-white gills and stalk. Both the flesh and stalk of this mushroom are brittle. Emetic Russula may grow singly or in groups. They are often found in the woods growing in mosses. They are abundant during July to October.

The Emetic Russula's cap is usually cushion-shaped to vase-shaped, with an incurved margin, and is smooth yet sticky. The gills are broad and attached. The stalk is straight and slightly enlarges at the base. It is off-white in color and has a wrinkled texture. The spores of the Emetic Russula, when magnified, are elliptical to oval. Most russulas look alike. They come in a lot of varieties, and a lot of them are red. That's why it's hard to tell one from the other.

Emetic Russula is considered poisonous. One of the symptoms of ingesting this mushroom is vomiting. Hence, it is also called vomiting russula. It tastes very spicy, acrid, and hot at the same time. Other symptoms attached to the sickener are nausea, abdominal cramps, and diarrhea, which may appear a half-hour after ingesting the poisonous mushroom.

False Morels

False Morels come from the family that falls under the phylum Ascomycota or sac fungi. It is likened to the true morels of the genus Morchella; that is why it is called a False Morel. And similar to Morchella, False Morel also belongs to the Pezizales. However, that group is subdivided into three families: Morchellaceae, Discinaceae, and Helvellaceae.

False morels are mushrooms with wrinkled and irregular caps, which are often described as saddle-shaped or brain-like. They come in colors ranging from black, gray, brown, white, and red. One False Morsel species called the bid red false morel, or Gyromitra caroliniana, is known for its reddish cap. It's also called the elephant ears, brain mushrooms, and Arkansas morels. False morels are abundant in the woodland grounds during spring, fall, and summer.

Conclusion

It may be surprising, but mushrooms are a significant part of our diet. From common button mushrooms for pizza, to the porcini mushroom that makes your favorite risotto dish so rich and delicious, we owe many of our culinary pleasures to these humble fungi. But how do you safely and accurately identify which mushrooms are edible and which ones may kill you?

The first step is to take a deep breath. Don't panic- if someone gave you a wild mushroom, you should be fine; it's only dangerous when they're raw or uncooked as this increases the risk of contracting mycotoxins (deadly poisons found in some species).

Once you're calm, take a closer look at the mushroom.

Mushrooms have three parts to them: the cap, stem, and gills. The cap is the 'head' of the mushroom, and it is usually this part that you eat. It's also usually where most of the mushroom spores are found. A cap can be convex (that's when it's round), flat or angular with cracks or folds in it. Some mushrooms have white or grey caps, while others are brown, yellow, or even pink!

The stem is what connects the mushroom to whatever they're growing on. Stems vary in size and shape but are usually very obvious. They're often darker than the cap, sometimes even hollow, and maybe smooth or fuzzy. Stem texture can help you distinguish between fungi family trees (so stay tuned for next week's article on mushroom families).

The third part of a mushroom is where the gills are located. Gills are what make a mushroom a member of the group Basidiomycota, which includes about 90 percent of all mushrooms. Gills can range from being hardly noticeable to almost completely covering the cap, so if you're unsure, look carefully at the underside of where the cap meets the stem. If you find gills, then you've identified a mushroom!

But what if you don't find gills? Make sure to look for tiny bumps under the cap of your mystery mushroom. If these bumps aren't gills, they're probably pores, which are like tiny holes dotting the underbelly of the cap. These pores can be white or grey and are often pearly looking.

When it comes to mushroom identification, size matters, you can take a picture with your smartphone and enlarge it on your computer or use a magnifying glass, but every mushroom has specific characteristics that will help you distinguish it from all the rest.

Just like the personalities of people, mushrooms also have their individual personalities. Every mushroom is not the perfect fit for every farmer. You first need to understand why you want to cultivate mushrooms. Is it because you want to eat the fresh produce? Is it to enhance the beauty of your garden or because you are thinking of starting a business?

Cultivating mushrooms can be extremely satisfying for those that have a genuine interest in them, and I presume, as you are reading this book, you are one of the people who really care about mushrooms.

We all know the toxins are building up in the Earth's atmosphere. The waste materials dumped from modern factories are responsible for this. The amount of oil spilled into the ocean has endangered sea creatures and the water. Nowadays, conscious people are thinking about ways to clean the waste off the face of this Earth. Here again, mushrooms are the answers to our prayers. Mushrooms have the strange capacity to grow on waste. It can transform the oil and chemicals into food, thus cleaning the environment in the process. Mushrooms are now used to clean the oil spills on the ocean beds.

Printed in Great Britain
by Amazon